Goodnight Mr. Vincent van Gogh

Lindsey Doolittle

Illustrated by survivors who have
lost a loved one to suicide

FH BOOKS
Kansas City

Goodnight Mr. Vincent van Gogh

Lindsey Doolittle

Illustrated by survivors who have
lost a loved one to suicide

Copyright @ 2017 by Lindsey Doolittle

Published by FH Books Kansas City

All rights reserved. Except as permitted under the U.S. Copyright Act of 1976, no part of this publication may be reproduced, distributed, or transmitted in any form or by any means, electronic or mechanical, including photocopying, recording, or without the prior written permission of the publisher.

Book Design by Gary Barber

Printed in the United States of America

For more information, visit
www.abovetherug.com

For my late husband,
Brett Doolittle
- and -
for anyone who has lost a
loved one to suicide.
It is not your fault and
you are not alone.

Opal Louise was in trouble at school one day.

Connie Bohannon-Roberts - Age 73 - Graphite
Illustrator Connie lost her son Daniel. He ended his life at the age of 39 in the year 2013

She scribbled all over her desk with a bright red marker during the morning art lesson.

Allie Doss and Abby Glezen - Ages 36 and 19 - Watercolor & Collage
Allie lost her daughter & Abby lost her best friend, Sara. She was 16 when she ended her life in the year 2015.

At lunch she refused to clean up her tray.

Steven Arkin - Age 52 - Ink
Steven lost his son Jason. He ended his life at the age of 20 in the year 2015.

And to top it all off, she yanked her friend, Bonnie's, ponytail while standing in the afternoon restroom line.

Bonnie Swade - Age 69 - Colored Pencil
Bonnie lost her son Brett. He ended his life at the age of 31 in the year 2003.

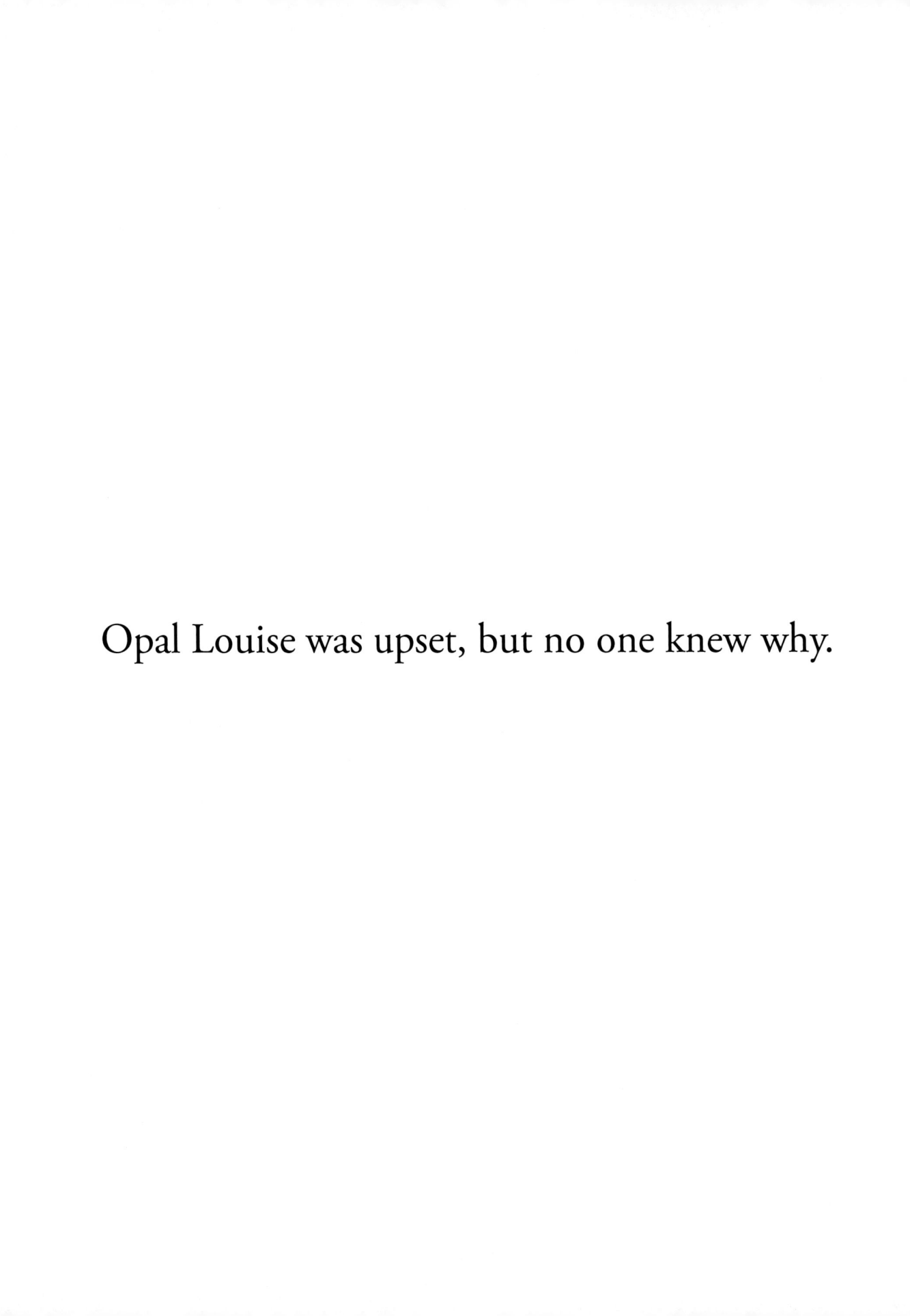

Opal Louise was upset, but no one knew why.

Stephanie Miller - Age 64 - Colored Pencil & Ink
Stephanie lost her son Billy. He ended his life at the age of 44 in the year 2016.

When Opal arrived home she did not kiss her father hello. She did not help set the table for dinner. And to top it all off, she ran to her bedroom and slammed the door shut!

Michelle Osborn - Age 46 - Colored Pencil
Michelle lost her brother Michael. He ended his life at the age of 47 in the year 2016.

Opal Louise buried herself tight within her covers on her bed and began to cry.

Minutes later, in the opening of her blanket, her mother's face appeared. "Are you okay Opal Louise?"

"Mommy, I miss Uncle Brett so very much. You said you would tell me how he died when I get older, but I just can't wait that long."

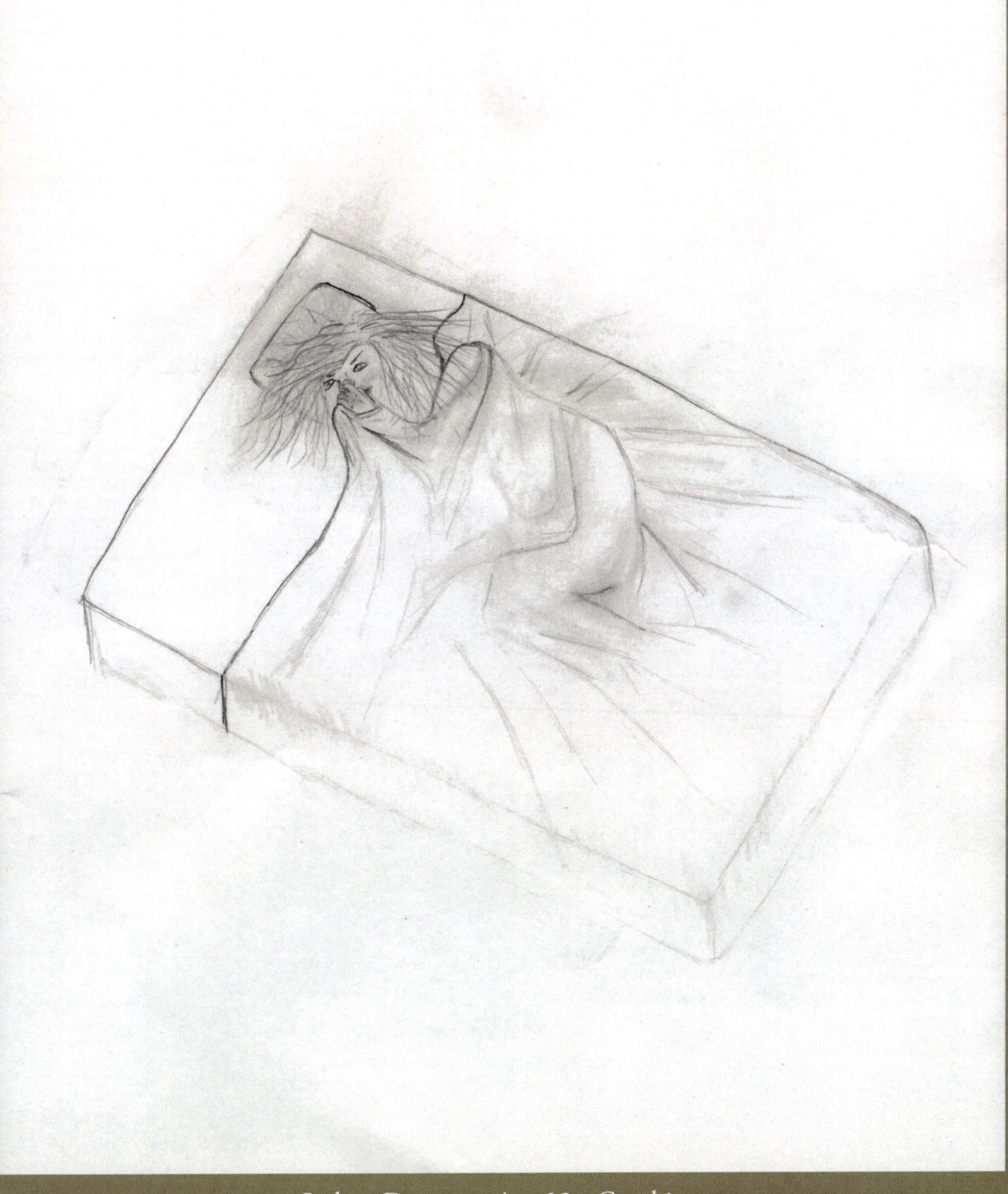

Joshua Duncan - Age 32 - Graphite
Joshua lost his wife, Mermaidia. She ended her life at the age of 27 in the year 2016.

Opal's mother gently lifted the covers, gave her daughter a tight squeeze, and walked over to the bookshelf. "Is this why I received a phone call about your behavior at school today?"

Alarmed by the news of the school calling her mother, Opal shouted, "Well, I just don't understand! You said he was sick, but I don't remember him having a cold or a tummy flu!"

Roger and Linda Cooper - Ages 72 - Graphite
Roger & Linda lost their daughter Julie. She ended her life at the age of 40 in the year 2013.

Her mother found the book she was looking for, climbed into her daughter's bed, and lay down beside her. Opal Louise wiped away the warm tears from her cheeks as she watched her mother flip through her favorite art book. She stopped on a familiar picture and asked Opal, "Do you remember who painted this artwork?"

"Oh yes! That is *Starry Night* by Mr. Vincent van Gogh. Our art teacher taught us that last year."

"Do you know where he painted *Starry Night*, Opal?" Opal shrugged her shoulders and shook her head no.

Nora Hosic - Age 11 - Colored Pencil

Nora lost her father, Paul. He ended his life at the age of 51 in the year 2017.

"Well Opal Louise, he was very sick and went to the hospital. When he looked out his hospital window one night, he painted what he saw in the sky and was feeling inside his thoughts. He was sick with sadness. Sometimes people become sick in their tummies, others become sick with fevers and coughs, and sometimes people become sick in their minds, which can cause them to feel very sad inside. It is called depression and it's not their fault they are sick. It is nobody's fault."

"Was Uncle Brett sad like Mr. Vincent van Gogh?"

"Yes Opal, your uncle was very depressed."

Greg Brostoski - Age 34 - Colored Pencil, Marker, & Ink
Greg lost his brother Michael. He ended his life at the age of 38 in the year 2014.

"But mommy, Uncle Brett seemed happy every time I saw him."

Her mother flipped a couple of pages ahead to a beautiful painting of golden yellow sunflowers.

"Yes Opal, you are right. Sometimes people who are very sad can hide it very well." She continued to flip through the pages.

Elaine Munyan - Age 57 - Colored Pencil
Elaine lost her son, Jesse, and her daughter, Emilie. Jesse ended his life at the age of 19 in the year 2009. Emilie ended her life at the age of 21 in the year 2015.

"And then sometimes Opal, people who are really sad do things that they wouldn't usually do if they weren't sad." Her mother stopped on a painting of the artist with a bandage around his head.

"Oh mommy, that's the picture of Mr. Vincent van Gogh after he cut off his ear! Did Uncle Brett cut off his ear too?"

Opal's mother set the book on her lap and hugged her daughter tight. "No Opal, but he did hurt himself."

Tom Phillips - Age 47 - Crayon, Colored Pencil & Collage
Tom lost his brother Bill. He ended his life at the age of 44 in the year 2011.

"Yes mommy, I know… he's dead." She desperately hugged her mother back. Nestled in her mother's warm embrace, Opal began to sob. "Didn't Uncle Brett know that I loved him? Did he not love me? Is that why he left us?"

"He loved you very much Opal; he just didn't love himself." With the palm of her hand she began to brush her daughter's tear soaked hair from her face.

"Mommy, I am so very sad that he is gone. If I'm sad, will I die too?"

"No baby, it's ok to be sad for our loved ones who are no longer here. Just promise me you will talk to me, your father, or your teachers when you are feeling sad."

"Yes mommy, I promise."

Amy Persechini - Age 58 - Paper Collage

Amy lost her sister Linda. She ended her life at the age of 64 in the year 2015.

Opal Louise hugged the book tight and flipped it open to the painting of *Starry Night*. She stood it up on her nightstand and turned on her lamp.

"Mommy, may I call Bonnie and tell her I'm sorry for pulling her hair today?"

"After dinner you can call her. How about setting the dinner table first? It's getting kind of late and I think we all could use a bite to eat."

Josi Puhak - Age 8 - Crayon

Josi lost her grandmother Terry. She ended her life at the age of 43 in the year 1993.

Quietly thinking inside her mind, Opal Louise smiled wide. She wondered if her uncle and the artist were talking to each other at that very moment.

She then shut off her bedroom light, walked over to her bedroom window, and to top it all off, whispered to the stars, "Love you Uncle Brett and goodnight Mr. Vincent van Gogh."

Lindsey Doolittle - Age 34 - Ink & Paper Collage
Lindsey lost her husband and best friend, Brett. He ended his life at the age of 34 in the year 2015.

Dear

Attach a photo of the one you lost here.

On the page before, write a letter to him or her.

ACKNOWLEDGEMENTS

To my family, friends, art students, and especially my nieces & nephews; Luke, Sam, Mercedes, Eliana, Alejandro, and Vicente. Mercedes, you woke something deep inside your aunt that night we laid in your bed and I watched you cry out for your uncle until you fell asleep. The love I have for you six and your uncle is the reason I wrote this book. Let this story be a reminder of your uncle's love he had for you.

And thank you to the creators of SASS (Suicide Awareness Survivor Support), Bonnie & Micky Swade. I hate how we met, but I am so grateful I found you both. Thank you for all that you do and the lives you touch. I don't think I'll ever be able to repay you for your help, but I hope this book is a start.

For each book that is purchased, part of the proceeds will go to SASS

RESOURCES

sass-mokan.com
SASS (Suicide Awareness Survivor Support) is a nonprofit organization that helps support survivors left behind after someone has ended their life. Their efforts unite survivors and educate the public on the stigmas of suicide and mental health awareness. They know that suicide is everyone's business.

speakup.us
The Speak Up Foundation (Suicide Prevention Education Awareness for Kids United as Partners) seeks to break the silence and reduce the stigma surrounding all mental illness and suicide.

itsok.us
The Greater Kansas City Mental Health Coalition is working to reduce the stigma of mental illness.

kchospice.org/solace-house
Solace House is a grief counseling center that supports children and families who have been impacted by the death of a loved one.

nami.org
NAMI (National Alliance on Mental Illness) is the nation's largest grassroots mental health organization dedicated to building better lives for the millions of Americans affected by mental illness.

suicidology.org
The mission of AAS (American Association of Suicidology) is to promote the understanding and prevention of suicide and support those who have been affected by it.

themighty.com
The Mighty publishes real stories by real people facing real challenges, including mental health.

suicidepreventionlifeline.org
The Lifeline provides 24/7, free and confidential support for people in distress, prevention and crisis resources for you or your loved ones.

ABOUT THE AUTHOR

Lindsey Doolittle is an elementary art teacher, author, mental health advocate, and suicide prevention activist in Kansas City. After the death of her husband, she wasn't able to locate any children's books on suicide for her young nieces and nephews. Plus, many of her students wanted to know what happened to Mr. Doolittle in the spring of 2015. She was faced with the question, "Should I lie and sweep this under the rug?" It became her goal to turn this devastating tragedy into something good, open, and honest. She became a regular attendee of SASS (Suicide Awareness Survivor Support) and now is a member on it's advisory board. SASS is a not-for-profit organization that helps educate the public on mental health awareness and provides support to the ones left behind after a loved one's suicide. SASS continues to teach her to not sweep anything under the rug, but rather to stay above the rug.

To see memory photos and to find out more visit
www.abovetherug.com.

Made in the USA
Columbia, SC
24 January 2021